Flying Above The Chaos

By: LaTonya Carroll

A Book Of Poems

This book is dedicated to my children Kedrick, Cedric, JaMesha, Josiah, Jimaur, and to the best uncle ever S.B. Carroll and to all of the countless men and women of God that were put in my life at such strategic times, that poured into me all kinds of support, your dedication of faith is outstanding. I hope this book gives you confirmation knowing that you acted out of love and faith. I am forever thankful that you didn't waiver when God spoke concerning me. To God, my kids, and all the people God used to stand with me, I love you all!

TABLE OF CONTENTS

ACKNOWLEDGMENTS

My greatest appreciation goes to our
Lord and Saviour, Jesus Christ

He is with us now and forever more and
through Him only all things are possible

"When destiny and purpose comes together, there's a shift coming that words can't explain. I don't live on purpose, I live for purpose."
LaTonya Carroll
online@www.walkinginmydestinyministries.com
.

Foreword

There are times when life can become this stream of steady flowing chaos. Intense breakouts of oppression against the peace of hope, prosperity, and love. In these times I have learned to fly like an eagle over a raging storm, it may toss you here and there but nevertheless remembering that I like the eagle, have wings that can soar above the raging chaos. Unlike the eagle's natural pair of wings mine are spiritual and have even greater ability to soar and defeat the purpose of the storm by flying high above all its chaos.

LOVE IS CALLING

I'm in a real dry place heavy burdened lots of
critical thinking desperate despair just to keep
me from sinking

Praying for breakthrough searching for a word
Keeping myself connected spiritually even though
sometimes church people are so absurd

Asking for forgiveness while on bended knee
Are you really listening God or is it just me

I'm waiting to see because I want to be free I find
rest knowing that my Lord never sleep nor slumbers

He holds my hands he knows my future
life is uncovered like the rising of the morning sun Love
is calling you, Love is calling you, your new day has
begun

"Situations can become extreme to the point where it's totally unexplainable. In these times are when you must depend upon something or someone with a deep level of assurance. I always can trust to find hope and peace in our Lord and Saviour, Jesus Christ"

I NEED YOU LORD

Lord my heart is heavy burdened and my spirit has been broken Asking for your forgiveness for the heard and the unspoken

the enemy knows my past but my God knows my heart even my worst's sins couldn't keep us apart

sometimes I may stumble but You won't let me fall Your love is calling me and I'm taking heed to its call

I need your direction I'm praying for favor to hide all my imperfections help my faith to increase and let my will decrease

Your word is a guiding light and a lamp unto my feet I will forever serve You unto that glorious day when we meet

"I have found rest and peace in knowing and believing who He is. I am encouraged and uplifted knowing what he has done for me and what he will continue to do for me."

WHERE DO I GO FROM HERE

Where do I go from here needing more and more of You every day where do I go from here wishing I could live this moment of life on instant replay

where do I go from here where the promise of God is so great where do I go from here when everything in the past seems like a mistake

where do I go from here sitting at the feet of heavens great

do I just keep resting in that secret place keep longing to see You face to face my life is in Your hands I'm trusting not letting go knowing that for my life You have a promise and a master plan

"I believe the enemy work in levels, using everything he can find to come against you at the best wrong time. When you believe what God has said concerning you and your situation, you have the power to change your situation and outlook. Eventually overturning what was meant to systematically harm you. Believing Gods best is for you, breaks the system the enemy is using to come against you."

DELIVERANCE IS FOR YOU

Asking myself why over and over again
telling myself no way before the end

secretly wishing for that big fairytale happily ever
after ending really not believing all the hope I've been
prayerfully sending

traveling this rough road on life's giant highway I'm
completely fed up of self and doing things my way

this is not like every time before if this is really
happening to me it is just what I've been praying for
deliverance has just walked into my open door

"Believing is one the greatest things that has ever happened to me. Everything you ever hoped and prayed for you had to first believe for. How can you pray and hope for something you don't believe. Unbelief and doubt will keep you from receiving the blessings(eternal life, healing, deliverance, prosperity,) of the victory Jesus won at the cross."

WALKING WITH GOD

When I'm walking with God I am beautiful my best me when I'm walking with God I walk boldly believing I receive and the Lord blesses me

when I'm walking with God my words are so bold, real and true I sing with an angelic voice that feels like its multiplied but that's not me Lord that's really just you

walking with God will take you into His holy place if you follow

as I sit behind the veil His glory is too awesome to consume the aroma is so sweet sweeter than the sweetest perfume

"I have been met with challenges that have led me to some chaotic times and moments. In these times, I have had to rely upon my God even the more and walk with him in a way that is keen, focused, and deliberate. In order to walk with God, you must walk like God. You must put on the whole armor of God and agree with his purpose and his will."

LOVE'S GLORIOUS OUTPOURING

Rose petals of love falling into pure refreshing
waters

nothing like the aroma of glory from my untold
story

I am in awe of His fragrance the more He gives
the more of Him I want

I need His love because its taking me higher
and higher

like a never ending fire consuming me with Its
power until I'm a remnant as pure as gold and
now my untold story is not untold

"To love is the greatest commandment . Real love is not ignorant or harmful. One that is without real love, is one that is without peace. One that is without peace, is one that is without hope. One that is without hope, is one that is without a tomorrow. Watch what you fall in love with because it will become a part of your tomorrow."

MOTIVATION

There comes a point when I have to find my motivation when I've conquered all of life's current situations

I take up my wings follow the winds of the Holy Spirit and Its shifting me higher into this consuming flow of God's love

His love keeps bringing out the best of me delivering me from the rest of me then It lands me in a never thought of place

right in the middle of my destiny

"Like the eagles and even the birds, the more they believe the higher they can go. Once it takes off and starts to reach unthought-of levels you can't catch it unless you have its ability. The more you believe, the more you will receive, and the higher you can fly. Once you start flying don't worry about what's behind you. Stay focused on where you are going. You will have time later after you arrive to your destiny, to come back and give a hand to those who haven't learned how to use their wings to fly."

FLY WITH ME

Top corporations couldn't keep me there
wasn't a party being thrown that could celebrate
with me

all of the gifts that you could ever bestow upon
me couldn't take the place of the greatest Love of
all, the only Love that ever really loved me

I'm riding high with Jesus taking flight while
your keys are still in the ignition I can't explain
this feeling the world doesn't have a definition

but He's given me a dream and dreamers
don't just dream they live their life through a
beam of Light that's shines through them so
bright

while walking in that Light things aren't so
tough even when it's a fight because no matter
how rough in Him is your delight

He's tastier than the sweetest things you know
even as I'm writing in this flow I'm being led by a
One Man's show

He's putting it down because it's time for us to get with His plans for a better people a better world even a better land

no one can do you like Jesus have you ever heard of a Love that so great that the deepest sea couldn't fulfill it the angriest man couldn't kill It

It will take your mind on a cruise give you a dream you could never loose and even when you snooze He treat you like a new pair of shoes

He walks with you and breaks you in keeping you close by even when you sin

if we could really go deep right now and focus in on the love of God, Agape love, the love that heals the love that compels to every situation

and know that God love us so deeply if we could see that clearly we would be a better nation......and that's my peace one love

The End

Flying Above The Chaos

ABOUT THE AUTHOR

LaTonya Carroll is a native of Houston, Texas where she lived until 2011, then moving to San Antonio, Texas. She is an inspiring gifted literary professional who didn't always see writing as her career of choice. She has always had the desire to sing and be an entrepreneur of some sort and after pursuing several business ideas she decided to seriously explore her inner being to see what she had been purposed to fulfill. It wasn't long after that when she began to notice her ability to inspire and impress through her way with words. That started the journey and ultimately gave her a new song in her heart, to write about her experiences and everything she was feeling. People were touched deeply by her considerate, caring and kind words of sentiment. It became clear to her that writing would be the first project that she would embark upon. Through this project a ministry has been birthed out called "Walking In My Destiny Ministries", here she will be able to use her platform in a way to inspire, uplift, and encourage people from all backgrounds, generations and denominations.

* 9 7 8 0 6 1 5 6 8 5 3 8 0 *